EVERY CHILD COMING TO AMERICA

Manuel Hernandez

Every Child Coming to America
Copyright © 2022 Manuel Hernandez

All rights reserved. No part of this publication may be reproduced, distributed, or transmitted in any form or by any means, including photocopying, recording, or other electronic or mechanical methods, without the prior written permission of the author and publisher, except in the case of brief quotations embodied in critical reviews and certain other noncommercial uses permitted by copyright law.

The introduction and stories from previous high school students have been published with the expressed written consent from the authors.

Front cover design by Graphic Artist Alejandra Gamboa

ISBN: 978-1948812375

Printed in the United States of America

DEDICATION

I would like to dedicate the book Every Child Coming to America to my wife, Maria Ortiz Rodríguez. Besides being the mother of our two children, Jose Manuel (Joey) and Josue Esteban, she has been by my side for more than thirty-five years. I married her in Puerto Rico. Just a year into our marriage, I convinced her to relocate with me to New York City. There, she gave birth to our oldest son. Then, only after three years in The Big Apple, we moved back to Puerto Rico. In Puerto Rico, our youngest was born. Thirty years later, I once again relocated with her to Central Florida. It is unusual for a woman to go through so much instability, especially when it comes to her dwelling place. I have been blessed to have her still with me by my side almost a decade into the Florida experience.

Maria, my love, this one is dedicated to you for all the time you have dedicated to me and my children. In-spite of the craziness of my ambitions and passionate zealousness to make a difference, you have always been there. You are my stability and the reason I am probably still mentally sane.

"Te amo nena!"

TABLE OF CONTENTS

Foreword	7
Introduction	11
Guide Questions used for the Scholarship Essay Writing	17
Blessed! by Paola Quiñones	21
A New Beginning by Danielys Coriano	41
A Long Path for A New Beginning by Alexander Echavarria	51
A Race Against Time by Haniel Reyes	59
The Dream by Alondra Rivera	63
The Best Time to Rebel by Karla Luzardo	65
Like a Butterfly by Isabella Adames	69
The Third Strike by Waldir Miranda	73
About the Author of the Introduction	76
About the Author/Editor Manuel Hernandez	78

FOREWORD
by Manuel Hernandez

In the 1950's, my parents joined hundreds of thousands of Puerto Ricans that moved into cities like New York, Philadelphia, Newark, Chicago and other metropolitan cities in the North and East of the United States. Seventy years later, Puerto Ricans are once again crossing the ocean, but this time they are calling Central Florida their home. In the twenty-first century migration, Puerto Ricans are being accompanied by Venezuelans, Colombians, Ecuadoreans, Mexicans, Hondurans, Dominicans, Salvadoreans, Cubans, and others.

Hispanics have the largest population growth in public schools in the United States. By 2030, 40 % of the K-12th grade population will be students whose native language may not be English. Registration data from the *National Student Clearinghouse* reveals a 5.3% decrease in the number of Latino/a undergraduates in spring 2021 compared to this same time in 2020. According to The Chronicle of Higher Education, the total number of first-year Latino/a students dropped 20% in the fall 2020. The numbers are welcoming when it comes to population growth, but in education, they are disheartening, staggering, and alarming all at once.

As more and more Latinos come to the United States, the educational opportunities are not available as their will to work, determination to succeed and the search for a better quality of life.

Instead of the "unskilled and uneducated" (Dr. Eugene Mohr, ***The Nuyorican Experience***) today Hispanics are teachers, doctors, lawyers, entrepreneurs, engineers, and other professionals including the working class that arrive with a strong sense of urgency to withstand the lack of educational gateways available to us all.

Sociologists predicted the great exodus from the Caribbean, Central and South America to Florida, but no one anticipated the terrifying effects of Hurricane Maria, and more than 100, 000 plus Puerto Ricans who relocated to Orange and Osceola Counties (Florida) at the end of 2017 and the beginning of 2018. The stories of these families and others must be shared and told for future generations to come. **The secret of their success dwells in their stories**.

These families moved to Florida looking for a better quality of life, and a fresh start for a new beginning. Because their first language was not English, they registered in schools with a great desire to learn the language but with developing English language skills that was met with academic challenges generally designed for native speakers of English. Many parents come academically prepared but limited English language skills and the lack of professional certifications in their professional fields deny them the opportunities available to us all.

The educational system is not totally equipped to receive students from different countries that carry a different set of cultural values completely different from the ones encountered in America. When the curriculum core is revised each year, there is no guarantee it will include a mirror for those who are relocating in

Florida and other states with increasing number of second language learners. According to American anthropologist, Margaret Mead, "Learning to speak a new language fluently depends largely on establishing genuine communication with the speakers of that language." This will occur when the speaker demonstrates an understanding, respect, and perhaps even empathy toward the culture represented by the language. *Every Child Coming to America* is a testimony of how much English language skills can be developed once culture is represented and reflected in their new-found educational experience. As a result, the pathway to America is portrayed vividly in their own words and according to how they experienced the journey to the new world.

In the acculturation process, students grow silent as they internalize the experiences of the new-found culture. In *Every Child Coming to America*, their voices come alive. These are their stories; told by ex-ESOL students themselves who arrived with hopes, dreams, and much uncertainty, and graduated from high school with a clearer vision and purpose of the present and upcoming days ahead.

The stories published in this book were submitted as scholarship essays in an application for a scholarship. With a clear and present understanding of the writing process, students are taken through a three-step culturally relevant journey. **As a result, all the students who submitted the essay or a modification of it received a scholarship**. In some cases, full-ride scholarships. As a complement for teachers and students, I included guide questions used to facilitate the process of writing a winning scholarship essay.

INTRODUCTION

Every Child Coming to America
by Dr. Tony Báez

I love reading the writings of young immigrants who come to America because of circumstances they may not control, and they quickly develop views about this country and its promises and tell us about it. Although disadvantaged, they achieve relative success in their young adult lives –despite the hurdles they encountered.

The essays in this book are by high school-age youth who look inwards and to the future. They are young people that give you their most personal, and often soul-searching descriptions of the challenges of arriving in a different educational system, a different language and culture, and who survived and attained relative success. These are essays of struggle, of climate and economic devastations that prompted departures from loved homelands and family, of fears, doubts, culture-clashes, and of wondering-if-I-will-make it; and they are also about the realization that one must continue to pursue dreams and take advantage of all opportunities –as all the now-published authors of these essays can speak eloquently about.

I was impressed by the sincerity and intimacy of the stories, even though some authors may not go deep enough into the educational struggles in their new schools, which adversely affect them and the less fortunate Latino students in a state like Florida; a state that some of us know is not friendly to immigrants and the economically disadvantaged. These stories also reveal future writers and scholars. The story on Hurricane María is great documentation of the effect and trauma of that climate disaster – they are pieces of gold. While some of us may not politically agree with the political vilifying of Venezuela by a United States whose economic embargo hurts more the people than the country's so-called misgoverning, we must see beyond that.

The stories that are included in this book are by young people victimized by the political battles among adults who pay no attention to the trauma, despair, and disruption of the lives of the young. Further, the authors of these essays are individuals who are academically more capable than others, regardless of what caused their displacement to Central Florida, and they also seem to come from more stable homes. Regardless, they tell stories that deeply affect us as we read, and they are evidence that the stronger you are in your language and your cultural and social consciousness, the greater your capacity to overcome academic and social challenges.

But there is something that runs through the stories of these young authors that cannot be underestimated. What made the most difference in their lives is that when they came to America, aside from their social and educational struggles at the beginning, they found friendly and profoundly committed individuals who told them they could overcome anything. They found a Club, "Coming to America" (CTA, as this club has become known to many). They found a Manuel Hernández: a courageous teacher that started the CTA, provides it with enormous continuity and personal support, and serves as counselor and advisor to the young people that commit themselves to it and its goals of making every young person survive and succeed. It's his baby, and this is his way of giving back by showing profound commitment to young people. They know he is authentic and believes in them and their potential, and that he is there to help them shape their dreams and plans for their future academic and personal success. He will do this despite what happens with his own future, his battles with his own school's officials and political and policy figures who he constantly approaches asking for their help to support CTA.

CTA is as a must for schools and every community for all kids coming to America. Hernández is the champion of these young adults. He knows they are making a new home for themselves –as will be shown in their stories; and he gives them hope, and lots of time, because this is an essential element in showing the caring and warmth needed to those adversely affected by social and often political circumstances. They found in him *cariño y confianza, y mucho corazón*. These young authors advance themselves through their essays, but they also honor and show great respect for his ways. I could go on.

Today, the young authors of this and other CTA books are being recognized all over their community. The Osceola Board of County Commissioners celebrates them; they are interviewed in television and radio; they speak at numerous school and community events; they speak to teachers and administrators when attending professional development conferences; they travel to other parts of the country. In summary, they have become stars and are held in the highest esteem. Surely, all this adds to their academic and personal growth, and all because they join the CTA and have evolved with the club into a lot more than an essay writing circle. It is a CTA that provides them with support and opportunities they would have never had without it.

I am reminded of the romantic pedagogues that in the past century were as dedicated to the young. They promoted student-centered learning that fostered their creative capacity. Schools that would provide activities that engaged the young in changing their own community for the better. For instance, in Uruguay, Dr. Jesualdo Sosa, published several pamphlets and then two major books of poems, one of 180 poems in 1938, and another of 500 poems in 1945, that were written by his students in a rural district. He had them writing extensively in his schools. These publications changed the lives of his students. Earlier, in the 1920s, Chilean educator and Nobel Prize winner, the poet Gabriela Mistral, joined the Mexican educator Jose Vasconselos in a huge literacy campaign to reduced illiteracy in Mexico. Mistral prepared scores of young students to teach literacy, mentor other young and adults, and engaged the young in writing curriculum specifically dedicated to the advancement of women in a country dominated by a male culture. Both Sosa and Mistral fought heroically against those that try to stop them, and eventually managed to get the writing of their young creative minds into the curriculum of schools. Even today they are celebrated in many Latin American countries.

There are other organizations in this country that publish the writings of immigrant students. But there is something special about CTA. It is all-around embracing of its members in support of their dreams and aspirations; it engages them in their community;

and it causes the educational, media and political institutions to celebrate and shower them with opportunities. The result: these young authors become better human beings who may give more later to society as adults. Hopefully, they will join Manuel Hernandez in the struggle to make America more caring and committed to its young. Let's applaud CTA for its unique way of turning the young adults that join this club into successes and brighter possibilities for the future.

MANUEL HERNANDEZ
Author/Editor

Guide Questions used for the Scholarship Essay Writing Process

Before:

1. What circumstances and/or situations paved the way for your family to move to the United States?

2. Describe your country of origin. Culture. Landscape. Nature. Politics.

3. When was the first time you heard the words "we're moving to Florida or we're moving to the United States?" How did you feel when you heard about the relocation?

4. Why did your family make that decision? Who specifically made it? Mom? Dad? Did anyone oppose the decision? Who? Why?

5. Who were the protagonists of your story? Who were the antagonists? Why? Explain.

During:

1. What was your last day/week/weekend in your country like? How did you feel on that specific day? What memories do you have of the last hours?

2. When did you leave your country? Describe the day, time, hour, and circumstances.

3. Were there any last-minute conflicts? Explain.

4. Who took you to the airport? Did you cross the border? How?

5. Who did you leave behind? How did you feel about leaving him/her behind?

6. Describe the trip to the airport/border. Any problems your family had on the way to the airport/border?

7. How did you feel when you got on the plane? Or when you crossed the border?

8. Who did you think about on the flight? Who was the last person you said goodbye to? What was that like?

After:

1. Who picked you up at the airport/border?

2. What did you do on your 1st day in America?

3. Where did you move? Miami, Orlando, Other cities…

4. With whom did you live with? Cousins, friends, etc.

5. How did you feel living with others you were not accustomed to living with? Were there any problems with those whom you lived with? Explain.

6. When did your parents register you in school?

7. Describe your first day in school. How did you feel? How do you compare your old school (your country) and new school?

8. What were some of the problems your parents had in Florida? Employment? Housing? Language? Culture?

9. Was there anybody that helped you adjust to living in Florida? How did he/she help you?

10. What problems did you have? In school, with your parents, etc.

11. How do you feel now? How have you adjusted to school? Do you feel welcomed in America?

BLESSED!
Paola Quiñones

The week the deadly Hurricane Irma brushed the east and north of Puerto Rico, electricity was cut off, and lightning stormed and turned the night sky to a reddish-brown with patches of blue. It had my family glued to the windows watching with child-like wonder and in anguish as the hurricane slowly passed. Irma just barely touched us, but its closeness left us wondering about our continued missed direct hits.

My dad, who worked for the government as CIO of the Department of Agriculture, worked for the governor's office. He was the Coordinator of the Emergency Management of the Agriculture Department Committee. He wanted us to help giving out coloring books and other toys, pillows, blankets, and watermelon to all the refugees who had been shipped and flown in from the Virgin Islands, and other close islands who suffered from Hurricane Irma. However, we needed to help stock up and clean the house to prepare for Hurricane Maria. The rapid forming of hurricanes was not a rarity to the islanders of Puerto Rico, and we were experts in scavenging the right provisions for a hurricane and cleaning the surroundings of our houses to prevent injuries from hammers flying around.

After we escaped from the claws of Hurricane Irma and during the weekend, we traveled to the south of the Island to visit and help my grandparents from both sides of my parents to prepare their houses and get ready for Hurricane Maria. Neighbors were drilling wooden planks to doors, hurricane-shutters on windows, and praying that Maria didn't blow away the beautiful palms and the trees that bloomed red, yellow, white, and blue flowers. We had just been through Irma, but reports reiterated Hurricane Maria's potential danger, and we prepared for the worst. It was characterized as a catastrophic hurricane of magnificent proportions.

Then, after enjoying the best brewed black coffee I've ever had, specialty of my grandfather, and a nice meal made by him as well with vegetables and pigeon peas he cultivated from his backyard and land – high in the mountains of Villalba – we said our goodbyes and drove back to my hometown. Along the way, my parents spoke about the part of the family that lived in other sections of the Island. We were so troubled about Maria's current course. Because the hurricane was expected to leave us without electricity for a long time, my dad purchased a generator. This was a category-four hurricane, and the prognosis was terrifying. My dad spoke about how it would be once the eye passed through my hometown, and how my dad would be called to work the moment the hurricane left the Island.

The day the hurricane was predicted to hit Puerto Rico the clouds were rushing by and a light sprinkle of rain came and went along with the blazing sun that made the day feel suffocating. We took our usual shower and dried the dogs, made a final sweep of the house, and sat back, watching a live feed of the governor addressing the natural disaster from my dad's computer. Later, at about 5:30 p.m., winds began to pick up quite the speed that instead of the whistle that I'm used to, they sounded like whips ricocheting inside a long tunnel, each louder than the last. Then as expected the electricity was cut off, but we still had clean water running, and the winds turned consistent and insistently picked up their speed to the point where our precious palm tree out front was perfectly tilted to the direction of the wind and trees swayed dangerously fast. There were patches of green in the sky from all the leaves that were swept from their trees.

I was awakened from a nap to the sound of trains savagely passing by the front of my house, only to realize that it was the mix of wind and rain that caused the terrifying sound, and we couldn't see the houses across the street. The windows began to rattle loudly, almost busting out, the dogs began to howl, and the windows on my room hurled open, letting water in. We were trying to calm down the dogs, and I tried to dry my room the best way I could, and my parents told me that while I was asleep the wooden roof of our backyard was ripped off and destroyed into separate planks, leaving only the wooden frame and pillars. Toys, seats, gallons, cans, anything, and everything flew into our backyard with such force that we thought the back door was going to fall. The tool shed was lifted off the ground; its doors blew open, but since my dad anchored it to the ground it wasn't going to fly away. Every sound heightened to the point where we couldn't hear each other talking. It was terrifying!

My family told me that the back door was leaking liters and liters of water, filling the house at a fast pace. We threw towels around it and tried to stop the water, but the towels were drenched in seconds when they touched the floor. The tube that drained the roof was placed directly on top of the wooden roof that flew away, and the water rushed out the hole it left, falling directly on the back door. My dad searched for a tablecloth and placed the mat in a way that only a small portion of the water filtered into the house.

Around two or three in the morning, I grew sleepy, but the urge to use the bathroom was bigger. However, the plumbing under the house that connected to the bathroom collapsed two months ago, that led us to build a bathroom from scratch at the front of the house – to this day still under construction – but at least it had a functional toilet. My mom accompanied me, since every sort of animal was trying to get inside the house, which meant rats were everywhere. Officially, my worst experience ever, and I didn't know what I was most afraid of, the hurricane raging in front of my house or the rat that scurried behind the toilet.

In the morning, the winds lowered their speed, but kept their steadiness, and rain kept pouring. It was a strange calm moment. My dad decided it was a good chance to close the gate that broke open during the hurricane, but my brother got distracted, and Robin, one of my dogs, ran out. My dad chased after Robin down the street while my sister held on to Zully, my other dog. We glanced to the other end of the street and saw water streams rushing down the intersection, spilling into our street, getting closer to our house. "If the water reaches the front of the house next door, grab your backpacks, and we go to our neighbors across the street. You all prepared a backpack, right?" My mom questioned as she opened the door to let my dad in. My dad told us that we were lucky to not have water already inside our houses, which the neighbors at the right end of the street were taking water out of their houses by the buckets, and as he walked back to our house, he saw hurricane-shutters zooming through the air. However, my dog was extremely happy to have gone out, mid-hurricane, gotten himself wet, and annoyed Zully to play with him by jumping on the white couches.

During lunch, the calm moment passed, and the winds came stronger than before. My mom connected a small barbecue gas to our miniature grill, while I whisked pancake mix with milk, vanilla extract, and two eggs. I buttered a pot, handed it over to my mom, as well as the pancake mix, and we tried to make pancakes inside the house, until the smell of gas was too much for my siblings, and we had to throw out the mix, opting for cereal with boxed milk, and cheese sticks on the side. Meanwhile, my dad was in the back trying to push rubble to the side and move the generator to a safe place where it did not get any more water. Since the hurricane was still passing, we couldn't turn on the generator in fear that it would blow up.

The following week was spent cleaning and moving all the waste from the backyard to the front of the house. We filled empty bottles and gallons with rain and water that was accumulated in the cooler to make our food on pots using the gas-pumped grill as the stove, and my dad contacted every person he knew to be in the capital. He asked for people to move the fallen cement light posts, traffic lights, phone lines, and unclog the sewers to filter out the stuck street-water. They told him that they would work as fast as they could but not to expect a fast response, as they were receiving emergency calls from all over the Island.

A week after that, the streets were free to roam but the excess use of gasoline for the cars and generators caused monumental, nine-hours-long lines at gas stations, seventy-seven cents the liter, but only a gallon per family. My dad spent eight hours to get us a gallon of gasoline for the generator, coming home with sunburns. Families spent hours under the scorching sun with a few bottles of water waiting to buy their share of the valuable gasoline and groceries. Food was scarce as only two or three small grocery stores were open, and even then, the food and water were rationed; some only permitted one gallon per family, other no more than four, or a box of water bottles, and the meats had to be bought to be made the same day, since there was no electricity to keep them from rotting. Unless we dunked the meats in buckets of salt, but my mom did not want to feed us excessively salty food.

One day, my dad took us out of the house and drove around to buy groceries, and to see the damages of my hometown, Caguas. I remember the rows of houses with all their house supplies on the sidewalk, people pushing water and carrying buckets of water out of their houses, and the video of the apartment complex's parking lot under water. The dirty water had reached a level where only the top of the cars could be faintly seen. A law was passed that prohibited the sale and consumption of alcohol, and another restriction law that placed the entire Island on house arrest; no one is to be seen out and about at seven in the night until six in the morning.

I spent my nights cuddling water bottles, without a blanket, nor a pillow, and with the windows open, trying to keep myself cold. The heat was intense, no wind, nor a light sprinkle of rain was felt during a whole week. As well, we were losing our patience with a family of rats used the pipe that drains water from our backyard as a home. The worst was when one of them had successfully found a way to enter my mom's room, and we had to close off that section of the house completely, which happens to be the easiest passage to the bathroom out front, otherwise we would have to go outside and enter from the front. Field trips were taken to the bathroom, each person had a job; one with a broom, another with a bat, the other with a flashlight, and another keeping a lookout for thieves that used these vulnerable moments to strike, whilst one of us bathed. During the day we would watch downloaded movies on my mom's computer until the battery ran out, then we would play monopoly for the tenth time, or lay on the cold ground, re-telling wonderful and comical memories of adventures in our Island.

During the next week, anxiety seemed to have been prominent at home, as my dad had begun to plan a flight for us to live with our aunts in Florida. He said that we would all get sick if we continued to live like this. He didn't want us to live like this, but I didn't want to leave him to live like this either. However, the airports were closed. No one could leave, and no one could come. Suddenly, as if some sort of miracle, my grandparents, and my dad's father, drove up to the front of our house. We were all surprised at how they came all that way to Caguas unharmed and smelling fresh. They said that their house in Villalba was protected by the hill behind them and the tall house next to them, and they only lost electricity, not water, though it came and left. On their way, all they saw were trunks and stumps where trees used to be, but that the grass possessed a lime green color, and they brought donuts, guayaba pastries for us, and bread pudding for my mom. Sadly, they couldn't stay the night, and drove back to Villalba before the sun had set.

During the weekend, my dad called to work and asked for a free weekend, because we planned to visit our family in the south, and they accepted by telling him to check on Villalba's governor who didn't call the capital to report the town's damage and needs. On our way out of Caguas, we saw the roof of houses and basketball courts blown away, baseball park bleachers also blown away, more and more missing traffic lights, and the remnants of huge, ancient, and majestic trees, either without branches, and others were ripped out of the ground by the roots. I cried at the sight of all the waste and damage the hurricane produced. It was unbelievable that even in this conditions people went to work, money was still needed to keep food in the house, to keep their houses from being taken away, and I realized that I too had to give my part in this.

Due to the absence of trees, the ground now took the delight of all the sunlight and water that once was only received a fraction. The mountains that once were covered with dark and light green trees were now covered with lime-green grass, which accentuated the mold of the mountain, and I couldn't help but awe at the bright-colored mountains that contrasted well with the patches of brown it had. Meanwhile, my parents argued over the decision of turning on the windmills of Santa Isabel during hurricane Maria, or not. My mom believed that they should have been functioning because they would have generated an immense amount of electricity, and the south would have been with light. My dad believed that they chose right in not turning them on, as the windmills could have suffered a great amount of damage, and even though they were able to withstand winds of great speed, the windmills were tilted. That if Maria were to pass once again, the windmills would collapse.

One month later, the island-wide curfew was changed; no one could roam the streets after nine at night and until five in the morning. The crime rates were surprising though. Such a devastating hurricane, leaving people vulnerable to thieves, but instead of being compassionate towards others, they had the audacity to break into people's houses, destroy most of their belongings, and steal valuable possessions, such as the generator. My mom, siblings, and I were scared one night, because it was ten, my dad hadn't come back from work, and there was a group of boys walking down the street, pointing their flashlights into houses, whispering between them, and they stopped right in front of my house. I considered that they wouldn't be stupid enough to jump our tall fence, and so we waited in silence. Until a car pulled in, they hastily got in, and drove away. Thank God, they proved me wrong.

Work had begun, and everyone that could receive the call from their jobs, or heard through the radio their company, had to wake up early in the morning the next day, and make their way to their respective jobs. My dad started before the rest of the population, but now, he left the house before my siblings and I could wake up, and arrived at near midnight, after we had gone to sleep. There were three days straight, when my siblings and I didn't see him, and though I understand that they need him at work, but there were times where I needed him there.

A few weeks into October, my mom was called by her workplace, the UPR. My dad proposed that he could take us with him to work, and at lunch, my mom would come to pick us up. That day I was nervous as my dad kept repeating that the U.S. marines were working, and that we shouldn't stray from him. We arrived at the convention center, and immediately we saw a group of marines with brown bags. We laughed at easily recognizing the grocery bags, and the countless boxes of sodas and bags of Snickers, Twix, and chips. My siblings and I followed my dad inside, and I didn't know where to put my eyes. There were so many soldiers, everywhere I looked; it was mind-blowing at the hustle of countless foreigners helping to restore main resources to my Island. My dad and his team included as well.

We couldn't be near the work, so they situated us in a far corner. We weren't complaining though; the air conditioner, the unlimited supply of fresh water, and a warm lunch was enough for us to keep quiet, while we played "briscas", watched movies on mom's computer, and tried to keep our voices low when we would unconsciously laugh. I, since we were continuing our education in a Florida school, sometimes studied for the SAT, working on my reading time, complex math problems, and learned how to block out all surroundings.

The day of our departure came; we were nervous, happy, and sad at the same time, if that's even possible. The airports were extremely crowded, and the fact that I was traveling alone with my siblings, and a younger cousin, terrified me to an extent. What if I say the wrong things? What if I leave our luggage around? What if I suddenly forget how to speak English? In a panic, my mind could only visualize all the worst-case scenarios, but thanks to my parent's reassurance, I put on a confident façade realizing that my siblings and younger cousin needed me in this stressful episode of our lives. We were blessed, as many more Puerto Ricans to have this opportunity. I repeated to myself saying that if God gave me a new beginning, a reset button, I should take this new chapter of my life with hope, patience, and the strength to make myself a better person, friend, student, sibling, cousin, and a better daughter.

The toughest part of the trip was feeling the buzz run through my body as the plane increased its speed to lift off. There is no turning back now. This is it, a new neighborhood, a new school, new people, and new opportunities to make better decisions. I smiled at the thought of seeing a part of my family I had not seen in years. I cried at the thought of leaving my family, my friends, and my home behind. At lift off, I began wishing that the hurricane never happened, that all those nightmares weren't made, that all those people suffering, yet to be located, could be carried to safety, that the leaders of my country strived to make Puerto Rico stronger and better than before Maria came, and that the families of all who died due to diseases, water contamination, food poisoning, floods, and landslides, could find the comfort, peace, and compassion they deserve.

Once I reached Florida, everything passed at an extremely fast pace. I immediately registered at Osceola High School. My parents sent money to buy us proper school clothing, and the only problem I faced was the language barrier. I knew how to speak, write, read, and I understand the English language, but the sudden transition from an all-Spanish routine, to having to think my words thoroughly, became a primary difficulty. However, at because I was received with open arms and not being made fun of how I speak English, I felt relieved and made the experience of immigrating to the United States of America much easier.

In such a short period of time, I have been through so much. I already transitioned out of an ESOL Language Arts class into a mainstream Language Arts class. I am publishing this story in a book. Life is going so fast, and I graduate in 2019. This has all been so fast, but the outcome of the whole experience has boosted my confidence, and I strive to work harder, learn more and look forward to a future filled with great goals and dreams. I am blessed!

It was a given that what the loved one felt for their family cannot be replaced. Let it be the love for family the feeling that pushes you in the right direction. Keep you humble, honest, and empathetic. It's what has helped me persevere in many challenges. I am grateful to have a family that cares for me, cares about my pains, my worries, my present, and my future. They have proved this by supporting me since my first book presentation.

On April 4th of 2018, Coming to America was published and announced in a presentation filled with hopeful and joyful sentiments. I remember entering Osceola High School at six in the afternoon, dressed in a white dress lent to me by an older cousin, had my hair flat-ironed, and makeup fixed by the same older cousin. From afar I could see the Media Center's doors opening and closing as people entered, and entered, and entered. I saw big, professional cameras next to well-dressed people, and I instantly felt the nerves causing goosebumps to rise all-over.

Fortunately, my friends, co-authors of the book, shared a laugh and a smile with me. That relaxed me a bit. They all looked beautiful and as nervous as me, but we all pushed the feeling aside by the realization that we did it! We were publishing a book, which we all helped fill with our unique stories. Alejandra, Hayla, Danielys, Olga, Dayivet, María, Italy, and Alexander. I'm more than proud of them. To have seen them working hard by re-reading and editing their stories, using the English language as a tool to perfectly shape the core feelings in their stories, rather than a barrier. Also, the book's first edition authors were there! Whose stories inspired mine. My friends already met them, but this was the first time for me, and they were the loveliest of people that I had the honor of meeting.

The evening continued with an ecstatic mood. Mr. Hernandez spoke at the beginning, calling each of us to take our place in our assigned chairs up front. With shaky hands but firm voices, we each stood in front of the crowd, feeling goosebumps as silence overtook the room, and people awaited the stories. Those stories, that once were kept close to heart, never to be known, were now spoken with a courage, far from the crowd's expectation. The audience was moved to tears and followed each reader gracefully with an applause.

I am proud to say that April 4th will always be the date I was most proud of myself, and one worth remembering for years to come. I remember that my mom, my dad, and my siblings were all in the audience. After the presentation, I found my mom with glazed eyes, a puffy red nose, and the widest smile that will fill anyone with instant joy. She engulfed me in a strong, loving hug and told me she was proud of me, so did my dad, and that I had a gift. But I don't necessarily agree with her.

My story is special because it is mine and only mine. The sentiment, the episodes, the memories, they're mine. As well, Alexander's story is his and only his, Hayla's story is hers and only hers, and so on. I believe the true gift I share with the book's co-authors is the conviction we mustered to channel our most precious memories, our most vulnerable moments, and transform them into words. From words into sentences, into paragraphs, and finally into a story. To have our stories beautifully printed unto those pages was proof enough that after whatever hardships we had to overcome, we still had the overachieving spirit of the strong-hearted laborer. Still, our stories have way too many smaller stories intertwined and etched with the emotions and boldness of a rebel, that they might never end. I pray that they never end.

Thankfully, mine is all but finished. After April 4th, our book, our club, and our names were known by the whole school, and that opened a grand number of doors. Both for the members of the club, as well as for the teacher, Mr. Manuel Hernandez. We presented in countless other places, appeared in television, and we were recognized by the Osceola Board of County Commissioners. The day the Osceola Board of County Commissioners had planned to grant us with a certificate and a pin of recognition, was a tense day. Not only were most of us going to stand inside a court such as it for the first time, but we also witnessed how members of the Osceola community stood in front those commissioners and delivered petitions brimmed with such captivating and honest emotions. Their stories, their words were raw to my ear, they left me speechless, and breathless in certain times.

During the summer of 2018, my body knew that the time for my inner sloth to come out was here. But my mind was racing faster than a trained horse. The only thing I thought about was the future. Sincerely, it terrified me to think that my future was never certain. Anything could prevent my pursuit, tarnish my motivation, and – I pray to God it may never happen – disenchant me from my desire to grow, learn, and make my best mark in the world. I only wish to be good, do good, and preach good. Strangely, knowing that my future is uncertain excites me. Because to me it means that I own the liberty to build my path as I go.

Towards the end of the summer, specifically on July 24th, the club was invited to be one of the speakers at a "Building Pathways to Success for Language Learners" conference.

When I entered the room in which we were going to present, I almost fainted. The overly spacious room was filled with countless round tables, all occupied by respectful teachers and leaders. This audience was noticeably bigger than our previous ones. My friends and I all looked at each other with giddy smiles and some laughs here and there. We practiced, we reread our stories for any questions later, we walked up to the podium, and we relived our stories. Even after hearing theirs and my story multiple times, the heartfelt memories still brought me to tears, and I wasn't the only one.

As I looked around the room, I saw some teachers sniffle, wipe their tears away, covering their eyes as they exited the room, and others just smiled through the tears, looking up as each one of my friends read with their heart in their throat. The applause after we all spoke was deafening, it blew me away. The heartwarming comments and inspirational advices from the teachers and leaders also amazed me. I couldn't believe the amount of support we were receiving, and this audience was by far my favorite. They participated, asked, and just – I was in utter awe.

In contrast, throughout the summer I couldn't help but wish to always have my father in Florida. The countless flights he took from Puerto Rico to Florida and vice versa, the guards at both airports now know him as a regular. Thus, he got checked thoroughly every time. I realized my father became something like a businessman, and I laughed at the thought of my father wandering from airport to airport with a suit and a briefcase. Though he doesn't need to be a businessman to be respected, in my books. Ever since I was able to recognize my dad's sacrifices, he was my hero. Along with my mom, they both raised me to be strong and not give up, no matter the situation, to be insightful and decisive when faced with problems, to be observant rather than to always openly express my opinions, and to be the bigger person. Being the bigger person, I can't beg my father to leave his job in Puerto Rico.

If you could put a picture next to the definition of selfless, I will waste no time to staple, tape, or superglue my parents' picture. It takes a certain type of person to live in the conditions that my father lives in Puerto Rico, and it takes a certain type of person to keep the image of strength in times that challenge said notion. The elated image of my mother every time my father flies to Florida is worth a thousand words. In no way, can I describe the way my mother just lights up when he's here, the way my siblings suddenly glow in his presence. I can only describe the way my heart swells with joy, the way my mind flows with creative inspiration, the way my fears, my worries, and my doubts are waved away with revelation. It takes a certain type of person to be the bigger person.

I take these values, my family-grown and self-achieved values, and enter my senior year of high school. I have a nag in my mind that tells me this year will be filled with many more revelations. Revelations of those who are true, those whose words not only encourage growth but also become an asylum when I'm lost. Like my U.S. Government teacher, Mr. Saragusa, my English 4 teacher Mrs. Dixon, my AP Spanish teacher Mrs. Irizarry, and my previous English teacher, now mentor, Mr. Hernandez. Their stories of how they persevered in difficult times echo in my mind when I find myself in difficult times. As I said, the future is tricky and uncertain, not always full of good moments, but not all are bad either. Up until now, my life has had its rough bumps, but the rest of the road seems clear. My goal still is to enter a good university after I graduate, take care of myself as the responsible student my parents raised and find a career that circles around the values that I stand and will always fight for. I just hope I still feel this way at the end.

A NEW BEGINNING:
ONE WITH WISDOM FOR OUR FUTURE

Danielys Coriano

Just like any other Saturday. We went to mass like we did every Saturday morning. The only thing different was that my father could not go because of his work. We arrived at my house later that day. When we entered the house, my father had already arrived and was talking on the phone. I continued my way to the bathroom in which there were two doors, one that connected to my parents' room and the other connected to the corridor. When I was about to leave the bathroom, I heard the word "United States" through the door that led to my parent's room. As soon as I heard that word, I hurried my pace and went into their room. While my father was still talking, we all sat around him in bed waiting for the telephone call to end. It was like any other Saturday, but the telephone call changed our lives forever.

When he finished the call, we all observed him waiting for what he was going to say. He said: "An old friend of the family has offered me a job in Florida." As soon as he mentioned those words, my sister began to cry. Silence flooded my soul, and I did not know what to say or think. My father continued to speak and said it was not a sure thing, but he was going to consider it. We all came into the conversation a little more and then each one walked towards their room, and the topic was not mentioned until the next day. When I sat on my bed and analyzed those words, many things went through my mind. All my life, I thought I would live in Puerto Rico forever. I also thought I would graduate with my friends and make my life at home. I was afraid of change, but my mind wanted it. I wanted to have a new experience, to learn another language and to have new opportunities. All I had inside my mind was confusion.

    The next day and as almost every Sunday at my grandmother's house, a family gathering took place, and my whole family attended. All my cousins and brothers played with each other or talked, and the adults gathered in their own little world with their conversations. I helped my grandmother in the kitchen, and the smells of her kitchen reminded me of typical Puerto Rican food. I worried that with time I would not smell the fantastic smells of rice and beans, "patita" and fried plantains anymore, but I ignored my thoughts and continued to help. The smell of my grandma's beans was breathtaking. There came a time when my uncles, grandparents, parents, and some of the older cousins sat down to talk. My dad once again picked up the topic: "I was offered a job in Florida"; everybody began to give their opinions. Some said it was a good opportunity; others thought he should think about it before deciding to move. My father said that if he decided to move, he would move first, settle down and then send for us. Then, he mentioned some words that although he used them a lot, that day touched me more: "That is what God wants". And so, the days went by, and everyone knew it was just a matter of time.

    I went to school the following Monday. When I got there, I told my friends, and they also asked when we would leave and why; we continued talking all morning. When I entered classes, the subject was still in my head, and I literally could not concentrate on anything. It came and went-but in the end, I got distracted talking, and I forgot about Florida for a while. Days and months went by and the school year was about to end. The month of May arrived faster than usual, and the date was approaching when my father was going to "experiment". It was not our turn to leave, but the day was rapidly approaching. It was hard to think we would not be closer to family but as everyone said it would be for something better.

Nobody wanted the day to come, but it did. My father was ready to go and try it out in Florida. It was a day of nostalgia, sadness, and a whole universe of emotions. When my mind stopped to think about when he would come back, I realized it would be either to pick us up or to stay. But we already knew the option to leave was the one that had more weight and soon would be a reality.

During the month my father was away, he called every day and told us how he was doing, what the environment was like, what he liked, what he did not like, and so on. When I visited or saw our relatives, they already knew the news, and some said: "I am from Puerto Rico, and it does not matter what I am offered, I will not leave"; which drilled a hole in my heart because part of me did not want to leave but another urged me to leave. I still did not know why I felt like that. But as my father said, God was the only one who knew why and the purpose of things.

School ended in mid-May, and my dad was about to return, but we did not know exactly when. He kept it quiet from us all. Only my mom knew. We were all so nervous. One day at the beginning of June, my father came by surprise and asked us to prepare for our new journey. That was the beginning of everything. We were leaving. But that was not the saddest thing, yet my grandmother to whom I was very much attached did not want us to go, but I was too sad like my grandfather, but what could I do if I had no voice or vote of what my parents decided. I was just a typical teenage girl who only did what her parents wanted her to do. When we visited relatives during the summer, they asked us the typical question: "do you want to go?" Obviously, our quick answer was no, but I still had that part inside me that wanted to leave, but I did not want to admit it because I love my country, my family, and friends; it was difficult.

The day arrived, and there would be no return. The airline tickets were already purchased for July 6; the date on which we would arrive in the United States. We packed three days before the departure date, and it was very sentimental because you knew it was time to leave. The best or worst day came, but I did not know how to take it when we said goodbye. Everyone cried, but I wanted to be strong. I held back the tears, but my heart was shattered into pieces. Those hugs and big kisses were taking away a big part of me. A friend of the family took us to the airport. This would be the first time my brothers and I would get on a plane. We were so nervous. We arrived at the Luis Munoz Marin International Airport. We said goodbye to our friend, and we did the inspection and sat down to wait for our plane to take off.

We were extremely quiet, and suddenly a lady sat next to us to wait for the plane and as every Puerto Rican does; she began to talk with us. She told us that she was from Orlando but made her life in Kissimmee, and she continued explaining how her life developed outside of Puerto Rico. She reassured me that life was good in Orlando, now the question was: how would life be for me?

The time to get on the plane arrived, and we were all very uneasy. While we were walking around the gate, my sister continued to cry, and it was exasperating because those were her feelings and those of everyone, but I was stronger. I felt the desire to cry yet something stopped me from expressing myself; I did not understand why. We went in. My mother and my older brother in one row and my father, my sister and I in another. I sat at the window and as the plane started to move my sister cried. A big part of my heart was falling off as I moved farther away. It was inevitable. Seeing my island through the little window on the huge airplane, moving away a little more each time, broke my heart but at the same time I felt confident because I knew that God had a purpose for us. As the plane advanced through the runway, I could not take my eyes off that window. It was amazing. Puerto Rico looked so beautiful. The sea from above, the islands and clouds were very beautiful and all that distracted me from my reality.

It was a smooth flight through the clear blue skies. Even the clouds seemed miles away from our plane. When we were almost there, I could see the giant landscape people call the United States. A giant plain, great terrain or a single mountain was so different, but I was not in my country anymore, and I forgot that. The plane landed. We all got off. My sister's eyes were wet, but she was quiet now. We were stepping on a new land, and our lives would never be the same again.

When we picked up our bags, we waited a moment outside the airport until the daughters and the wife of my father's old friend picked us up. They hugged and greeted us very warmly. They talked a lot with us and explained many things about Florida. We moved in with them until the paperwork for our house was finished. We stayed in their house for about three days and then we finally moved into our new home. I was grateful because they helped us a lot. It was not going to be easy, but we had to try. My father got a job for our older brother. My mother got us ready for school. There was a lot of paperwork in the process, but our first day was just a few days away.

We arrived during school registration days. Although I was ready to embark on the new journey, my nerves were getting the best of me on the way to school. To go to do the paperwork, we were accompanied by one of the daughters of my father's friend, my sister, my mother, and me. When we got to the school parking lot and saw how great the school was, I felt I could not even begin. For a moment, I felt great pressure that I had to really "get on my feet" and tried hard to make my learning fast. My mother finished the process, and we went back home. "We are already registered, so fast," I said to myself. Then, the day came to buy uniforms, clothes, and everything else. The holidays were over, school days were approaching and suddenly the school's open house came by magic.

During that day, I was a little nervous yet calm at the same time. First, I took the talk in the auditorium and then we went to the classrooms where we would take each class. The first teachers I met were Mr. Hernández and Mrs. Carrasquillo. When I spoke to them, their presence gave me a lot of confidence because they spoke Spanish, and they were very respectful and cordial. I already knew I should not worry so much because I could understand some people because they spoke my language, but the pressure of learning English was still there. When it was time to sleep that night, my sister and I could not sleep at all. In our minds, the nervousness of the next day prevented us from getting any sleep.

As if nothing happened, the big day arrived. It was the most anticipated but unwanted moment. My mom took us to the first day of school, and while we were on the road all my family called us to wish us luck. That distracted me from the whole thing. Then, we were already in the doorway, and my desire for a new language and the positivism I felt disappeared, I thought I could not get out of the car. My mother, a great and beautiful person, gave me the strength I needed saying: "Trust in yourself and put all your worries to God, and everything will be fine". I took a deep breath and continued my path with my sister. Then, the bell rang, and everyone went towards their room. I met new people who made me feel safe because they spoke Spanish and had the same situation as I did: "We were Latino, immigrants, new to a culture, and separated from our mother country." Although I did not believe it, we had more in common, we all looked for opportunities in a foreign country.

The days went by quickly, and my confidence increased. It was difficult but not impossible. My English was improving, and more practice helped me. One day, Mr. Hernandez, to whom I thank very much for the opportunity, invited me to be part of the great club

"Coming to America". After consulting with my parents, I said yes, and I do not regret having done

it. At the first meeting, he spoke to us about the purpose of the club and about writing our story. In this club, I met great people and obviously young people and students like me with whom I had many things in common. They became a big part of me.

Finally, time passed, and my grades were going well. My vocabulary developed more and more, and I had new experiences every day. The club meetings helped me and made me feel part of something in this new world, to which I was already getting used to. I met new friends just like me from different countries. Each teacher with his or her teachings and anecdotes impacted my life in some way or another.

Now, I speak in the present and not in the past. I have become a different person with great goals to achieve. Changes are difficult and painful, but they lead to big things. With very little time in the United States, I have been able to get ahead with the support of my family, which I thank very much. Assimilation sounds like a long and strong word, but it is important to adapt to a new culture and embrace it to be successful in that new-found home.

It makes us better people. It is necessary we also know that although we are far from our homeland, family, and our people, we do not stop loving them. All the doors that opened in my life have a purpose. It is we have faith and put God first in everything because he will help us. We must be people who trust in ourselves. My story may not be as full of obstacles as other people, but I know I was able to overcome them at the time. This is the beginning of a stage full of opportunities, and I know that the processes have finished, but now I know that with strength and courage I can face them all.

The key to starting a new life is to gain wisdom and experience from changes and mistakes. Surrendering is not an option, getting ahead yes. I want all young people to who have dreams to go to the university, get a profession, improve their English, and every day exceed their limits and be a better person.

Exceeding the limits was what we experienced during the spring and summer of 2018. On April 4th, we had our book presentation. The Osceola High School Media Center was filled with teachers, relatives, and friends, and I was super nervous. After all the writing and rehearsals, it was now time to deliver the excerpt of my story. Every one of us was introduced by our teacher, Manuel Hernandez. He read a biography for each and added a special description for each one of us. Our limits were exceeded. Everything went well, but it was only the first of several presentations. We went to a library, read at a university, and even were named "Distinguished Citizens" of Osceola County.

I never thought I would ever be an author of a book. This dream was one that I was not too sure about, but I did it; we did it. All nine of us who together with our teacher were able to describe in simple narratives what our journey of Coming to America was like. As I completed the first semester of my senior year, I could not help wonder what the future was going to bring in 2019. This was, is and will continue to be a new beginning; one that has brought a lot of wisdom for our future.

A LONG PATH FOR A NEW BEGINNING
Alexander Echavarria

Everything started when my dad received a call from his cousin that lived in the United States of America. They talked a lot, and she told my dad she was going to buy a ticket for him to come to the United States. He only needed to say yes, and he did. That ticket was for February 4th. He told us one week before he left that he was going to leave our beloved Venezuela. Everybody was sad, but he decided it was the best decision for his family. It was a silent drive to the airport. We said goodbye to him, and he got on the airplane. A few moments later the plane spread its wings and went high up in the sky. I will never forget that phone call.

After some connections and delays, he arrived at the United States a day after he left. We had mixed feelings about his departure. We knew that he did it for us, but we wanted him at home. However, he received a lot of strength to move forward with his plans for a better quality of life. As the days passed, he called us almost every day through face time. Sometimes I didn't want to talk to him because I really missed him. Other times, I saw him on the screen and was heartbroken because my father was on the other side, and I couldn't do anything to give him a hug or just touch or talk to him. The distance from my dad taught me a lot. It taught me how important my father was in my life. Although I did not see him often when he was with us in Venezuela, he was an essential and valuable person in my life. It was his sacrifices that got us through difficult times.

I was distraught but, in some way, it was good because our relationship grew and strengthened. Well, the days passed, and he started working as an automobile mechanic. During those days, he called us less because he worked many hours. In addition, he took buses and traveled to work on a bike. He woke up at 5 o'clock a.m. to go to his workplace. Weeks passed, and he saved money, and soon rented a house. After four months, he called my mom and asked her if she wanted to come to America with my sister and me. My mom thought about it and agreed to make the trip to America as well. We were all speechless and happy with the news and the idea to join our dad in the United States.

Some people say the journey to America starts when you get on the airplane. I don't agree. The journey begins when you hear that the family is moving to the United States. The thought of leaving your country of birth is breathtaking. We had four weeks to prepare everything for that day. Everybody was content because we were leaving the country for a bright future, but some friends and relatives were sad because we were leaving the country we were raised in, the country that saw us grow. My entire family lived in Venezuela. The journey was just about ready to begin.

There were a lot of rumors about how long it would take us to become American citizens. Some said it was eight years, and others said it would take more, but we were mentally ready to embark on the journey to Florida. I knew it would be difficult, but I dedicated some time to study the American culture, and I felt I could adapt to a new culture and a new way of life.

I said to somebody that I left my country because it was the only option I had, but it really was not true because I could have stayed with my grandma in Venezuela, but I wanted a different future. So, what was the first step? Move to the United States, and that was what I did. My accounting professor in my old school said that life in the United States was not easy. I said to him: why isn't it easy teacher? He said you paid taxes for everything. If you wanted to get a job, it was hard. Even renting a house was not easy. You needed to have good credit to buy whatever thing you wanted. He also said that everything was different, the culture, the language... there were more difficulties, and the list went on and on and on. But he told me "Good luck Alexander, I know you can do this; you will be successful in that country" after he told me all that I was a little nervous and scary. But that didn't stop me, and I realized everything was just part of a life process. Nothing could stop me from what I had already decided!

Everybody says life gets tough when you relocate. I don't agree with that point of view. I think life gets more interesting because you encounter new things and experience things you never thought you would have a moment to enjoy. Life is marvelous. Life teaches you things that may hurt you, but sometimes the thing that hurts you makes you mature and grow.

I'll never forget my homeland, the land of my birthplace. It is like a poem that you love. It is unforgettable, a country that notwithstanding all the problems-you uncover the picturesque country, a country that wherever you go is pleasing. It is the most gorgeous country in the world. Our music, culture, and food and all the things that I can see, that's what Venezuela represents for me.

In the morning, the sun is a rainbow of many colors. What about the sounds? How about GAITAS (Christmas music in Venezuela) and the voices of people passing in front of my house. And how about the birds singing and a lot of noises that compound the Venezuelan sounds? Amazing! Unforgettable! What about my beloved food that I just loved with all my heart? I thought about all of that for example: "arepas", "hallacas", "pabellon", and "cachapas", also sweetness has to be in a country of enjoyable people like "dulce de lechoza" or "dulce de cabello de angel" (Venezuelan food) and all that and more are the taste of a country that has a variety of gastronomy. That's why I love my country!

On June 15th of 2015, we started our journey at 4:30 am. It was a quiet and cool summer morning. My uncle, my cousin and a friend of my aunt picked us up. The journey was about eight to ten hours long. I got on the car, and I started to sleep. Halfway through the trip, I opened my eyes and the first thing I saw was a beautiful and unspeakable landscape with a bright sun I will never forget, a grass full of a combination of two colors yellow and green, birds with colors that brought me joy.

We stopped after a long ride to eat breakfast. It was the best breakfast ever in my life! It was awesome because it was what I just loved, an "empanada de pabellon con una malta bien fria". And then we were on our way. At that time, I didn't sleep. The only thing I did was think and analyze why I was moving to America. What was the reason why that was very important? Another thing happened; I remembered everything: my house, my street, and my friends. All that was in my heart. Tear drops fell from my face. We stopped to eat lunch. It was very delicious. And then we continued our journey after arriving to San Cristobal, Venezuela. After three hours, we arrived, went to the hotel, and slept to take a long rest for the next day.

On the next day, we crossed the border from Venezuela to Colombia. On the border, some soldiers revised our luggage to see if everything was ok, and they took some things, but we stayed quiet. We passed that, and then we went to the hotel where we stayed until the next day to go to the airport in Cucuta, Colombia. The next and big day arrived, and we all prepared for the process we were all going to go through.

So, we were at the airport, and we all went to the front desk to give the tickets, and luggage after that the only thing left behind was to get on the airplane and say goodbye to my grandma. That was the worst part for me in the journey, but I had to be very strong to say goodbye. My grandmother was very special to us. She accompanied us in such a long and treacherous journey. She is my inspiration, and she is in my heart every day, and every moment she is in me. She always laughed with me. Thanks, grandmother, for being in my life forever and ever. You form a very important part in my life. Without you, I don't know if I could ever exist.

I finally said goodbye to my grandma and gave her a big and memorable hug. That moment passed, and we were on the airplane and started to fly. I was in the window seat I loved because you can see the sky, the clouds, the sun and the sea. We arrived in Panama to take another airplane to go to Orlando Florida.

When I stepped on American floor, I remembered why I was there and what my purpose here was. We waited for my dad. I saw him, and I ran to give him the hug I was waiting to give him. And then we went to a restaurant to eat. We were exhausted, but we were happy because we were fine and safe and all together.

I came to the United States just for one reason, a bright future.

Coming to America was the best decision that I ever made in my life. There are no regrets, and I will never get tired of thanking my dad for taking the challenge of providing a better future. Here at this moment, I can say that America has provided me with good help and an excellent chance to move on, learn and realize all my dreams.

I have learned how to see myself in a mirror. I have learned how to succeed in whatever you want. The only thing you need to do is set goals for yourself and to get stronger. One day after school, I was at home, but I was feeling horrible. I was crying, and I did not want anyone to see me crying, but the only thing I knew was that I was emotionally hurt, and I didn't even know why. I wanted to talk to somebody or hear a voice and the two persons that came to my head were my grandparents. I immediately called them. I talked a lot with them. I just needed to hear their voices. I remembered their house. I loved that house. I remembered when I was in their home. I remembered when I was with my grandpa doing a "trompo" (spin) of wood. That day was awesome, and I played with him. I talked to him about it all. Distance helped me out in various things. It taught me how to appreciate times with my family. And really cherish moments in my homeland.

From the first to the last day of school at Osceola High School, I have been making a difference. There have been feelings of loneliness, unfairness, and worriedness; mixed feelings that come when destiny and determination come into the arena of life and success. Writing and presenting my story to other people were the most significant and memorable moments in my life so far. I will never forget the first time we presented our book Coming to America. And then after that going to the public library in Kissimmee and later being recognized by the Commissioners because they wanted to highlight our triumphs as second language learners. Getting recognized was one of the best moments in my life. Then we went to Ana G. Mendez at the Orlando campus and in that moment Mr. Hernandez and his wife gave us our medals for being in Coming to America. But the most important event that impacted me was the keynote conference at the Embassy Suites. We were the keynote speakers in front of one-hundred teachers from Osceola County. This presentation was the one that I liked the most because Mr. Hernandez gave me the privilege to share my thoughts, feelings and how I overcame my journey. These moments marked my heart forever and are also a memory that I will never forget.

Now that I am at the end of this journey in high school, I am very excited, happy, and blessed of my memories in high school. I speak in the present. I am senior in the FBLA club (Future Business Leaders America). I am in the Robotics clubs, and volunteering in Healing Touch Therapeutic Riding Center, and of course in Coming to America, a club that opened doors to a variety of opportunities.

A RACE AGAINST TIME: A NEW LIFE
Haniel Reyes

While growing up in Venezuela, I spent my time trying to take apart, fix and improve electronics, from my own toys to home appliances. When I had a screwdriver in my hands, I felt like I really loved what I was doing. As time passed and I grew older, my love for electronics grew deeper. Without being conscious of the passage of time, I was fast approaching the conclusion of my 11th grade. To top it all off, I was ending the year with the highest grades I had ever achieved. I knew then that my senior year was going to be my best year. Unfortunately, that was not the case.

Politics began to affect the entire country of Venezuela. We began to experience unscheduled power outages. As a result, sometimes when I got ready for school, the lights would go out. Other times, the lights would go out in the middle of class while I was at school. The power outages would occur at any time, day, or night. All too often, the power outages would cause classes to be suspended almost daily. These power outages did not only affect the schools, but they also affected markets, clinics, and every industry throughout the country.

My senior year in high school started on the wrong foot. However, I had faith that things could still change for the better. I refused to believe the situation in which my family found itself, would dictate my future. Teachers began to leave my school after the government created inflation by lowering salaries and raising the cost of living even higher. My parents could no longer afford to provide private education for me as the economy prohibited such a luxury. Rather than use our funds for private schooling, we agreed that other bills and food would take precedence over the indulgence of a private education. My dream of finishing the 12th grade became dismal because I had to leave school. I did not register in the local public school, as the public schools had become disastrous ensuing the exodus of the teachers. My 12th year of high school simply vanished along with my dreams of graduating and pursuing further education.

To help my parents with the economy of our family, I began working. I fixed computers, installed software, and replaced parts. My involvement in the field of computers and electronics reinforced my love for this area. Unfortunately, the situation in Venezuela worsened which made me look for another job with a fixed salary. At 16 years old, I started working at an ice cream store. While I enjoyed my job, I was not passionate about it and I knew it was not what I intended to do with the rest of my life. I did not feel fulfilled, and I wanted more, as I was aware that there was more to life than just selling ice cream. I wanted to do something important with my life. I planned to finish high school and then further pursue my degree at a university to study a major in computer or electrical engineering. I understood that it was not going to be easy, but I believed that I would overcome these obstacles to accomplish my dream. My only possibility to reach my goals was to leave my birth country because of the political and economic unrest.

Eventually, with the full support of my family, I started to research different possibilities in other countries. Amongst the countries I researched, the United States was at the top of my list. Finally, with the support, blessing and help of my father, we bought tickets and boarded a plane to the United States. We arrived in the United States on August 14, 2018. Without letting much time pass, the following day we began to identify the requirements and procedures to register for school.

A day later, I registered as a student at Osceola High School as an immigrant pursuing his dreams. There was now a new problem though. I discovered how expensive universities are in this country, which became a great disappointment for me. As a recent immigrant, I realized I would not be able to afford to pursue a college education in the country I had quickly fallen in love with. I began to research ways in which I would be able to attend college. I had never been a person who gave up without exhausting every possibility for a solution. One day, I heard something about the career center at my high school. I learned they could help me research options and guide me to make the best decisions regarding my post-secondary studies. Someone told me very good things about Valencia College and the opportunities Valencia provided to dreamers. I knew that with opportunities and my love for electronics, something good could occur. I started to research more about those opportunities.

During that time, my English Language Arts teacher spoke to me about joining a club he created called Coming to America. Besides writing and publishing personal stories, the club also became a bridge in the student's quest to go to college. I respectfully declined becoming a member because I had to study for four standardized exams and worked part-time to help my parents pay for utilities and essentials while we settled in the Kissimmee area. However, I agreed to collaborate and help him as a Teaching Assistant. Mr. Hernandez agreed to help me as much as he could in the pathways towards my dreams.

After an intense one-semester at Osceola High School, I received a full-ride scholarship. A month later, I received a second scholarship. I graduated in May and immediately started college that summer. It was a race against time! I relocated as a senior, learned how to navigate the system, helped my parents pay the bills and was accepted at the university with scholarships to pay for all my studies. It was a new life, so sudden, so fast but with a huge desire to make a difference and help others like me cross the bridge I crossed as a senior in a high school in Central Florida.

MY DREAM
Alondra Rivera

My room filled with the smell of pencils and paper and a desk by the window. A small garden outside and a plant for inspiration on my desk. A couple of books in other languages like Korean and Portuguese scattered on my bed and my luggage which were ready to go to any destination. My finances so well managed that I was debt free. My customers were happy and satisfied with my creation. I was interested in the fields of architecture and engineering. It was my dream, and I was never going to let go.

    I never knew that the dream was much more than what I had already planned for in my beloved Island, Puerto Rico. I was determined to take the dream with me to Central Florida, and I was not going to let anything get in the way of the aromas of my room and the garden outside my childhood home in the so-called" Isla Del Encanto". My interests became my heart and soul, and the memories of my relatives and friends in my "Isla" were the catalysts of a new way of life. I hated goodbyes but welcomed new beginnings. As I said goodbye to everyone, my mind was fixated in the future, and I shed tears and cried but looked forward to the challenge with new hope and determination.

    My dream was inspired by my godfather and the movie **Hidden Figures**. My godfather is an architect and since I was a child, he would always take me to architecture workshops to build and design buildings. On Christmas, as a present he always gave me good quality coloring pencils and a sketch book. The movie *Hidden Figures* vested my interest in engineering teaching me that you can also be an engineer regardless of gender and ethnicity. That movie empowered women and minorities to approach a field dominated by men.

    I wanted to create and design houses that were environmentally friendly. I wanted to be able to use my resources: technology and education to help other people obtain their dreams. It could be making their life easier, comfortable, and safer. During this school year, I hope to be more active in my community and achieve a greater number of hours of community service than my previous years of high school. To achieve my dream, I first need to serve and understand the needs of my community. Scholarships would help me take one step closer towards my dream. They will help me pay for college which will help me prepare, gain knowledge, skills, and experience to achieve my dream.

THE BEST TIME TO REBEL
Karla Luzardo

Waking up on April 23, 2016 was an interesting experience. It was time to prepare for our trip. I was used to traveling, so I did not feel sad while packing up; until I had to leave my home to go to the airport. This trip was different. I was leaving my country. Venezuela: the land of "milk and honey". Well, that's the way my parents lived it when they were teenagers. Venezuela bragged about its oil, and its seven Ms. Universes, but all that was gone. It was the best time to rebel.

I gave my grandma a hug and a kiss goodbye with hope to see her soon. I got into my aunt's car and began thinking about how it would be like to live in a beautiful house and go to school in the United States while looking out the window with "Eres mas" by Guaco playing in the radio. We finally arrived and went straight to check our bags and then get on the plane. As a 12-year-old girl I was excited about studying, since I knew that this is a land full of opportunities, and I was willing to give my all to achieve my dreams of a better future for me and my family.

There are about 5.4 million Venezuelan refugees worldwide according to (The UN Refugee Agency); I am one of them. Certain and unforeseen events threatened my family's safety in my home country. My parents introduced me to the idea of us moving to the United States. My mom faced persecution for opposing the Venezuelan government, causing our family to be concerned for the safety of our lives. With the dangers we faced by staying, my parents decided to move to the United States. While we buckled our seatbelts, my mind was already in a school in Florida. We arrived at Orlando's International MCO Airport, and some distant relatives picked us up, and took us to our temporary house, which would become our place to stay for the first three months. Those couple of months were difficult since living with people was not the most comfortable experience. Our values were not compatible with the people we were living with, and our way of life was totally different. Those first few months, I observed my parents struggle to find stable jobs, and the money we brought went faster than we expected. We were desperate to find a way out, so we started looking for options. One day we finally moved to our own rented apartment.

When I started my first day of school, I felt like another foreign student that could not find a comfortable place to be in. I also did not make many friends those first two years, which made my time here a little lonely. Inspiration was converted it into art. Every time I wanted to cope with something, I grabbed a pencil and got lost in every stroke. This passion opened many doors of recognition including participating in a county office contest where I was finalist. While art became important, so did academics and my intent for better options did not stop there.

I decided to apply for Dual Enrollment during my sophomore year of High School. I did not have guidance or enough support to totally comprehend every part of the program and when I asked my high school counselor about the DE program, all the answers I got were "are you sure you want to be in it?" and "this is a college level program." I was both ESOL and had not passed the FSA, so opinions like that did not take me by surprise. I know I'm not the only Latinx student that feels that way. I still felt capable, so I pushed it, and got in. It did not matter what people said or thought of me. I worked hard and I got in. I started participating more in the Hispanic community clubs in my school. I researched about some opportunities as a non-permanent resident. Every time I asked about scholarships, I always got the same answer which ended up being the FAFSA. Unfortunately, my options were narrowed to certain colleges that did not require permanent residency. I have come a long way as a student with no guidance. Working passed the difficulties is an essential skill for success. I am considered a "rebel" because I do not take no for an answer or listen to those who say, "You can't" or "You don't qualify."

I wanted to focus on the search for opportunities that could impact my future positively. Venezuela was now my childhood story, which was the foundation of my character. I wanted to have an impact. My migrating story reflects how I experienced many things and learned every step of the way. I am still in the search for new opportunities to achieve a higher education. Even if it takes me many years to do it, I will never fail to continue to pursue my dreams in this country. Every remarkable story has a major struggle, and mine is being a foreigner.

LIKE A BUTTERFLY
Isabella Adames

I've always admired butterflies. These incredible creatures can live everywhere, although they prefer warmer climates. They can be found anywhere throughout the world. These wonderful creatures adapt and, during their short lives, undergo a wonderful transformation, unique in the world of insects. They generate joy and happiness in everyone who sees them. When I think of them, I think of my life. I am like that. Although there have been some hardships along the way, my smile, positive attitude, and willingness to adapt and adjust to life have helped me be successful.

I was born in a small town in Venezuela. My parents taught me the value of hard work and instilled in me the values of respect, kindness, and consideration. I've always been a person with peculiar and specific tastes. I like broccoli for breakfast. I like to adopt insects and watch them grow. I like to compliment and smile at people. I like the smell of pine trees. I like the way a freshly sharpened pencil relaxes me. I like to read curious facts every day and try to understand the human brain. I am selective with my tastes, my social circles and, above all, my goals.

On the other hand, I am also a realistic person. I realized that my country had become a gray territory without joy, suffering from serious political, economic, social, and security problems. We were sometimes without water for twenty days. We cooked when we could because the electricity was also out for most of the day. Everything was and still is in chaos. People lost faith and hope because nothing they did, whether it was study or work, led them to success or even access to the most basic items. Healthcare and food became unattainable.

Seeing this was both sad and frightening, I knew we needed to make a change. I asked my parents to take us to the great United States of America. I was too young to understand how challenging this move would be. I only saw a plane leaving and imagined us up in the clouds, heading to a place where Mickey lived, and all our dreams would come true.

My parents finally decided to leave Venezuela after my father was diagnosed with Parkinson's disease because there was no medicine for him in my country. In 2019, we arrived in the U.S. with a suitcase full of memories. I left behind my grandparents, uncles, cousins, neighbors, friends, and pet. It wasn't easy to put everything in one suitcase and start the trip, but I remembered reading, "Sometimes plants need to change places to keep growing." I was excited about my new opportunities in America, but only a few months after arriving, I had to face the pandemic like everyone else. This made learning a new language very difficult. I listened to music and watched TV and YouTube videos. I felt pressured to learn quickly so that I could be prepared for my challenging classwork and the SAT. I felt rushed to learn so that I could give myself the best opportunities for college and my future.

Everything that I've experienced has made me who I am today. "We delight in the beauty of the butterfly, but rarely admit the changes it has gone through to achieve the beauty." I am that butterfly who has lived through many changes. I'm ready to fulfill my dreams in a country where democracy reigns. I embrace these dreams with hope and faith. As I imagine my future, I look to my past experiences. Seeing my hero, my dear father, sick and struggling, has inspired me to pursue a career in healthcare. I want to help others like him, and I know that through a career in healthcare I can do it. "If you do not live to serve, you are not good to live." This phrase lives present in my soul all the time. I am Isabella Mercedes Adames. In my culture, my names mean "the one who loves God" and "liberating woman," and I'd like to live my life honoring my names.

THE THIRD STRIKE: OUT OF THE BALLPARK
Waldir Miranda Salazar

Once upon a time, I visited Florida twice before relocating permanently. On the first trip, I came on vacation, visited the parks, and had a whole lot of family fun. The second time, I ran away from problems in my country. Completely different experiences that helped me see the world from different perspectives and helped me realize I wanted to fight for my future. My family and I came to the United States looking for a better quality of life because life seemed impossible in my beloved Venezuela. Two strikes but the third one was going to be the most significant.

Adversity, obstacles, and hardships knocked on our door every day in Venezuela. There was crime, violence, and political chaos everywhere. Relatives and friends were being kidnapped for ransom. Food and electricity were scarce. My parents decided it was time for us to leave before things got worse. I lived in Venezuela for fourteen years and for me the change was difficult, but I knew that for my parents it was going to be even harder.

It is painful to talk about my sister's death. However, my family's decision to move to Florida was another way of leaving some of the memories and pain of my sister's untimely death behind. Her illness and struggle to survive was a token for our efforts to move on and start from scratch.

The last day in Venezuela was filled with many contradictions. In my heart, I loved my country, but I saw no future for me in it. I relocated to the United States with my mom, my stepfather and my two younger brothers. Although we left many of our friends and personal belongings behind, we were still together. This was my third strike, but I was ready to hit the curveball right out of the ballpark. I focused and looked deep within, put my legs together and hit the ball with all my might. A third journey with a fixed sight on a bright livelihood and a better future.

Relocating to Florida began with decisions I needed to make to start moving towards the development of my dreams. First, I started high school in my sophomore year. Osceola High School was huge. It was nothing like schools in my country of origin. Second, I did research about the educational system and discovered what I needed to do to be academically competent. It was tough since I did not speak any English when I arrived. Last, I decided to focus all my energies on learning English. My sister's last image was always there, and focus was not always simple for me.

On my first day, I was very confused about everything that was happening, but when I got to my first class, I realized there were more Venezuelans, and I felt more comfortable with the environment. Time passed, and I became more involved in school and with better English I opened myself to more opportunities and challenges.

I have been passionate about medicine since I was little. Since I grew up in a medical environment (my dad, my stepfather, and my grandparents), which led me to dream from a young age with this profession. My biggest goal is to be able to study medicine and develop in other areas of this profession. Nobody said it was going to be easy, but I will strive and fight to achieve it, because I love medicine. I love the idea of being able to help people and save lives. I want to be a doctor, specifically I want to be a "pediatrician, childcare and neonatal intensivist".

Since I was a child, I have dreamed of following my father's footsteps. Today my dream is bigger. It is to be able to help save lives and build a better future for the next generations and improve medicine in some way. I want to be able to help people, hold my instruments and save lives. That is why I want to go to the university because it can be a turning point not only for my career but for the rest of my life. I need to walk along the pathways of my future. I am interested in becoming a mentor for other students like me who had to leave their homeland and move to America.

ABOUT THE AUTHOR OF THE INTRODUCTION
Dr. Luis "Tony" Báez

For over fifty years, Dr. Luis "Tony" Báez has promoted and defended the civil and human rights of Latinos and others, especially of children and youth affected by educational systems. In Wisconsin, he has promoted bilingual and multicultural education, and has helped established school and college-based programs, and other opportunities for the professional growth of Latinos. Further, he has promoted the idea that bilingualism and multiculturalism is good for all of us, and that we need more bilingual and dual language schools.

Dr. Báez is constantly learning about the great educators of the past and present, especially in Latin America: humanist thinkers who fought for schools that are based on a learner-centered pedagogy, as opposed to the austere and alienating focus on a pedagogy that suppresses the intelligence and creative capacity of the child, destroys the disposition to learn, and wrongly measures intelligence through standardized tests. This is an approach that has not worked. Dr. Báez has called for its end, supplanting it with arts, music, languages. Growth in reading, writing, math, science skills, and other skills will follow, he says. Similarly, he proposes a humanizing re-education of teachers, administrators, and parents to stop destructive and trauma causing child educating. He promotes a decolonizing pedagogy that rejects racism, sexism, injustice, and social inequality, and which embraces learning that is fun, promotes peace, not hate, a love for life, and a safe and promising democratic world.

Dr. Báez has a Ph.D. in Urban Education from the University of Wisconsin-Milwaukee. He is a scholar who has administer community-based schools, taught in schools and higher education. A former Vice-President of the Milwaukee Public Schools Board; former member of the Executive Committee of the Wisconsin Association of School Board Members; and former Chair of the National Latino Educational Research and Policy (NLERAP). He was Provost at the bilingual Eugenio Maria de Hostos Community College in Bronx (City University of New York); and Coordinator of the National Origin Desegregation Assistance Center at the University Milwaukee-Wisconsin. Dr. Baez has traveled to many other countries to speak on educational issues; is a constant reader and social critiques of literature and pedagogy; and plays the guitar, sings of social justice and performs Latino poetry. He is also the recipient of many awards including the Martin Luther King Heritage Award for Social Justice. In his name, the Wisconsin Association for Bilingual Education annually offers the "Tony Báez Leadership and Advocacy Award." In 2020, he was the recipient of the prestigious international OHTLI award by Mexico for his advocacy for the rights of Latinos and bilingualism in the U.S.

ABOUT THE AUTHOR/EDITOR
EVERY CHILD COMING TO AMERICA
Manuel Hernandez

Manuel Hernandez was born in Sleepy Hollow, New York in 1963. His upbringing was as diverse as his professional experience. He completed his grade school experience in New York, and his parents moved back to their homeland in 1974. From 1974, his lifetime experience has been a revolving door experience between the Island of Puerto Rico and New York City. He completed high school in Rio Grande, Puerto Rico in a school called Pedro Falu. He completed his Bachelor's degree at the University of Puerto Rico, Rio Piedras Campus in 1986 and finished a Master's in Education from Herbert H. Lehman College (CUNY) in the Bronx, New York in 1994.

In 1988, he was hired as an ESL teacher in The Bronx. As an ESL teacher in New York City, educator and author Manuel Hernandez saw that multicultural students wanted to learn, but classroom materials weren't relatable to their own cultural experience. Hernandez learned of the significant difference in the classroom when culturally relevant materials were introduced into the learning experience and how we all can benefit.

But "after an intensive month of 'Romeo and Juliet,' he understood that he had a major predicament in his hands. Determined to bridge that gap, Hernández discovered the power of authentic and meaningful relevant literature, which constructed bridges of understanding to teach his students to learn English, stay in school and pass citywide exams at the same time.

Fast-forward 2014, purpose called him to come to Central Florida and use his thirty-year teaching experience to facilitate language learning and get immigrant teens college and career ready. As the migration shift moved towards Central Florida, he knew he could use his initial teaching experience and "jumpstart" their academic experience. Florida had other demands, but it was a revolving door experience that had him "flashbacking" to NYC. After several years in Florida, he has been able to help open the academic doors that had been shut for many of the recently arrived.

He founded and created an educational program called Coming to America. Coming to America published its 3rd edition in March of 2019 and its first ever bilingual edition in March of 2020. The Coming to America book is a collection of unique memoirs which depicted the journey of Latino teens who arrived with hopes, dreams, and uncertainties in their particular and distinct young voices.

In 2014, Hernandez participated in a TEDx Talk (Connections) at Southern New Hampshire University. After six years, Coming to America has transformed into **Every Child Coming to America**, and the program that started in a local high school in Central Florida has continued its growth outside of the school community and has the potential to impact school communities outside of the limitations of the school boundaries in which it was created.

He is the author of four books, **_Latino/a Literature in the English Classroom_** (Editorial Plaza Mayor, 2003), **_The Birth of a Rican_** (Divine Purpose Publishing, 2021), the **Coming to America** series (four books, 2017, 2018, 2019 and 2020, (*Divine Purpose Publishing*) and **_Living the Kingdom with Purpose (English and Spanish)_** (*Divine Purpose Publishing*, 2017). He is the father of two boys, one, an adult, Jose Manuel (Joey) and Josue Esteban, a young teenage adult. He has been married for more than thirty-five years to Maria Ortiz Rodriguez.